THE VOYAGE OF ST BRENDAN

A.B. Jackson was born in Glasgow in 1965 and raised in the village of Bramhall, Cheshire. After moving to Cupar in Fife he studied English Literature at the University of Edinburgh. His first book, *Fire Stations* (Anvil), won the Forward Prize for Best First Collection in 2003, and a limited edition pamphlet, *Apocrypha* (Donut Press), was published in 2011. In 2010 he won first prize in the Edwin Morgan International Poetry Competition. His second collection, *The Wilderness Party* (Bloodaxe Books, 2015), was a Poetry Book Society Recommendation. *The Voyage of St Brendan* is published by Bloodaxe Books in 2021.

A.B. JACKSON

The Voyage of St Brendan

WITH ILLUSTRATIONS BY

Kathleen Neeley

BLOODAXE BOOKS

ISBN: 978 1 78037 566 3

First published 2021 by
Bloodaxe Books Ltd,
Eastburn,
South Park,
Hexham,
Northumberland NE46 1BS

www.bloodaxebooks.com
For further information about Bloodaxe titles
please visit our website and join our mailing list
or write to the above address for a catalogue.

Supported using public funding by
**ARTS COUNCIL
ENGLAND**

Cover design: Neil Astley & Pamela Robertson-Pearce.

Printed in Great Britain by Bell & Bain Limited, Glasgow, Scotland, on
acid-free paper sourced from mills with FSC chain of custody certification.

for the Fureys –

Martin, Áine, Robert

ACKNOWLEDGEMENTS

Acknowledgements are due to the editors of the following publications in which some of these poems first appeared: *Bad Lilies*, *The Dark Horse*, *The Island Review*, *Poetry*, *Poetry Ireland Review*, and *The Poetry Review*.

This work would not have been possible without a PhD studentship from Sheffield Hallam University in 2012 and the guidance of my supervisors: Steve Earnshaw, Maurice Riordan, and Chris Hopkins.

I am grateful to New Writing North for a Northern Writers' Award in 2016, and to the Society of Authors for an Authors' Foundation grant which allowed me to travel to Ardfert and the Dingle peninsula (including Brandon Creek) in April 2019. Thanks in particular to Maurice and Aileen Walsh of An Bóthar guesthouse for their hospitality.

Special thanks to Clara Strijbosch for detailed feedback on the notes section, Andy Ching and Andrew Neilson for feedback on the work, David Wheatley for suggestions on Irish names, and to Kathleen Neeley for being an exceptional collaborator.

CONTENTS

ILLUSTRATIONS

THE VOYAGE OF ST BRENDAN

Brendan

Brendan, son of Cara, son of Finnlug. Brendan of the Altraige, their lands north of Tralee. Brendan whose birth was foreseen in visions of woods engulfed by flame, in visions of whitefooted deathless inviolate brightbodied angels. Brendan baptised by Bishop Erc at Wethers Well, and fostered early. Schooled by Ita in her monastery at Killeedy and counselled by her thereafter. Brendan who messed about in boats on the blowy shores of Fenit Island. Brendan of legend, Brendan of books. This Brendan.

Called by the voice of newrisen God, ordained by Erc, he set about his own foundations: Ardfert, monastic settlement, camp of labour and prayer. Grain had its three homes: a barn to hold, a kiln to dry, a mill to grind. Pigs fed on autumn acorns. Blacksmiths, those ding-sounders, made ploughs. From workshops came cruets, vestments, vellum. As the poet said:

> Visitors flocked, and Brendan washed their feet.
> The guesthouse was a barn of souls in need:
> aspirants, penitents, paupers, budding martyrs,
> peddlers, druids, lords, professional farters.

Brendan, holy Abbot, mother hen. He put on the armour of faith and walked like an athlete into the arena. His diet was meagre: tree bark, herbs, and haws; the occasional hazelnut. His brethren called him Cruiskeen, for in virtue he was considered the full jug, the vessel from which all were replenished, and, in crueller part, because of his ears, two blockbusters, windbreakers.

Community wrongdoings were many and hourly, correction delivered by leather tawse. The oakhouse, the church, held song. For all this, Brendan was not at one. As the poet said:

Brendan's mind was braided, equal strands:
the Kerry bond / an ache for mythic islands.
His dreams rotated: sea's wrath, brave sail,
or yellow gorse and lambing fields in April.

His pet crow, Préachán, knew tricks and flipped latches. His pet fly, Quilty, was in truth many flies called Quilty over countless generations of the one original fly, or, some said, any fly whatsoever that flitted through Brendan's day, due to the cracked milk pail of memory and the lack of distinguishing features in houseflies. In this way, also, he avoided such grief as follows the loss of a precious companion.

His chariot had an admirable rumble, a high-born squeak, a deer-bolting rattle, the wheels iron-shod, the shafts holly-poles, the whole shebang drawn forth by oxen.

The Burning of the Book

Books were Brendan's love. At number one,
Amazing Tales, a vast compendium.
Within, he found the Mathematic Salmon,
the Manticore, the breath-defying Dragon.

The dog-head folks, called *Cynocephali*,
a godless bunch who play the banjolele.
The Arctic tribes who worship tiger seals,
their ice-hickle cities on wagon wheels.

The whale *Jasconius*, its mountain-back
all porcupined with oak, and elm, and ash.
And *Inexpressible Isle*, its ruined fort
with butterfly judges, Heart's Grief Court.

In time, this diet of ripe and rum detail
weighed on Brendan: he sickened, grew pale.
He craved, instead, a simple common sense
in keeping with his Rule of abstinence.

'These things,' he cried, 'are figments, folderols.
The truth is here, at hand: a linnet's carols,
Kerry mountains, Christ upon his hook.'
And Brendan made a fire, and burned his book.

The Boat

Brendan's dream was short. An angel spoke:
'The book you burned, that marvel-busy book
is fact not fiction. Abbot, hear my curse:
you'll sail abroad, prove wonderstuff on earth.'

On waking, flesh and spirit were engaged.
'Brothers, build a currach! Come, make haste!'
Fifty hides were bathed in oak-bark liquor,
one full year, the tanning spell for leather,

and waterproofed with stinky wool grease.
Carpenters raised a body, piece by piece –
gunwhales of oak, the rest of bone-white ash:
thwarts and ribs and oars, the single mast.

The hides were sewn, tacked on, an outer skin
whose reek made every Dingle dog a pilgrim.
And Brendan cried: 'No miracle of God
outshines this boat! I name her now – the *Cog*.'

Brendan's Meditation

In a hollow on the slopes of Sliabh Daidche, Brendan built an oratory of stone in which to meditate upon the journey to come. His neighbours: purple heather, rock samphire, sea thrift. Away to the east, the Three Sisters, their peaks rising like wave crests. Within, a reed mat for a bed, a lamp with oil of basking shark. Through forty days of fasting and prayer, he fixed his eye on the intolerable ocean as many angels came and went: some in flocks, black-spangled like starlings; a red-breasted sentinel, crowning the roof; the hunting hoverers who emblazoned the air at dusk.

The Crew

Fortified Brendan consulted stars and tides. Leaving day chosen, the *Cog* was carried on the shoulders of monks down to the creek's mouth. Sea foam choked the inlet. The boat was blessed, provisions checked: the salted fish, the water skins. Tears, tears for Ireland and the loss. The *Cog*'s crew, six chosen brothers, climbed aboard with Brendan.

Brother Robert: helmsman, hawkeyed, a hummer of tuneless hums. A nose for lichens, pollens, land. Prognosticating star scholar, sky-versed, a son of Dunmore East.

Brother Michael: the cook, from Cork. A druid of barley broths, toothsome treats, meal breads. Burly bigfoot. Plays the bones.

Brother Tom: carpenter, adze master, nailman. A Scot from Fort William. Strawberry blonde, wood-shavings curly. Grudge nurse, doomsayer, sour as month-old milk, but with his cat, called Shonnet, all doting sweetness.

Brother Seamus: youngster from Limerick, just two years tonsured, freckled as blue tit's eggs. Earnest of eyebrow, cub-curious, impossible slender fingers.

Brother Colm: gardener, true muck's ambassador. Broad-thumbed, ruddy, compulsive whistler. Tongue shy, though, and word-fallow.

Brother Aidan: scribe, vellum tattooist, wave stenographer. Old feller. Quill stash. Ink horn. Satchel. A martyr to his cramped right shoulder, his candle-ruined eyesight. Hunched, the way a heron can be hunched.

Shore Song

The mooring rope was untied from its rock, winds boasted of their existence, and Brendan's crow circled overhead with repeating, shingle-rough cries. His fly was somewhere busy on sheep's droppings. On shore, it was brother Robin who sang a farewell song, a song of lambs and yellow gorse, apple trees and morning lauds, as the *Cog* disappeared into the great unfathomable storm-riven whip-jawed ocean.

The Great Fish

Fair winds and wave-voice
       the currach speeds west
as Brendan's heart thumps
       an apple harvest

Arrow-fall gannets
       bullseye the sea-skin
on board all chatter
       high moods in a swim

A low-humped island
       where puffins might rest
unpeopled verdant
       furred with a forest

The crew drop anchor
       skip-scramble ashore
their hunger a hound
       with scent of wild boar

Brother Colm chops wood
       a kettle-fire struck
like a bee-stung hulk
       the island rears up

The ground faints away
       monks helter-skelter
the trees become masts
       pitching off-kilter

Mad dash for the *Cog*
        raise anchor set sail
the ocean a pot
        on furious boil

On the forward slope
        a geyser high-puffs
the island a whale
        great *Jasconius*

The creature dives down
        the wind gusting strong
Brendan's mind scattered
        St Dandelion

The Mermayd

At sea, the foxing playfulness of light:
sun dogs, halos, downsideups, fake sight.
One rainbow-day, big Michael raised alarm:
obscured by glare and swell, a creature swam.

Revealed at last, in heart-clattering view,
a fishtailed woman, vision true-untrue,
her upper torso mouse-haired, modest coat.
Wolf-purposeful, she circled round the boat.

Brendan scolded, 'Brothers, do not tremble!
Tom, stop gnawing that wooden spoon handle.
Our currach floats on salted Providence,
curried leather. Quit this flapping nonsense.'

In swift response, the mermayd (as she was)
flicked her tail, dove down, consumed by froth.
The gaping crew were famished or well-fed
as she gurgled profoundly from the sea bed.

Thirsting Souls

Night fell fast, the boat somnambulant.
Brendan's mind was fruit bats in a tent –
splashy footsteps, first, then solemn figures:
nine embodied souls with rictus features.

Brendan hailed them: 'Who saunters over water?
Neptune's boys or ghouls from Ballyferriter?'
'Neither,' answered one. 'We're stewards, butlers.
In penance we hike these chilly frontiers.'

'Bluish gentle sir,' said Brendan, 'what crime
compels you to perambulate the brine?'
'We never shared our masters' excess food.
Poor folks thinned. We failed the common good.'

Brendan took pity and prayed loud: 'Lord,
fresh water, please, for this itinerant horde.
Bless their lips, re-seed their barren throats.'
The nine drifted on, haunting the sea roads.

The Coagulated Sea

The *Cog* spins northwards
       bucked by rough seas
her sails fully strained
       like hounds on short leash

Six unlucky brothers
       cough up their breakfast
their garments bibs
       indecorously splashed

The storm's holy force
       the waves' war zone
the crew turn ashen
       flesh weak on the bone

As winds fall a notch
       their spirits grow level
until a wraith of mist
       swallows their vessel

Brother to each brother
       looks insubstantial
a crew made of gauze
       a composite fog-animal

The *Cog* stops rocking
       and lies dead still
the sound of snapping twigs
       the work of some devil

Clicks or a tick-tock
        the small voice of ice
coagulating waters
        moving at snail's pace

Brothers gaze in wonder
        ice plates or pancakes
flagstones and icebergs
        each with its own face

Mottled as mirror-glass
        or bubble-transparent
azure blue boulders
        a jewelled firmament

The *Cog* now encased
        it is Brendan who sees
a thin host ahead
        like spears or trees

To and fro swaying
        a multitude of masts
their hulls crushed
        by glittering mouthparts

Dig, brothers, dig!
        with oars and kitchen knives
the crew hack and hammer
        their second skin of ice

They lever the boat loose
        tooth from gum
Eastwards! turn east!
        cries trembling Brendan

The Cliff-top Monastery

A cry of 'Land!' A cliff face, iron ore red,
a monastery perched on top, gold-gilded.
The crew cast anchor, doggy-swam ashore
and surfed the scree slopes in buoyant uproar.

The summit gained, they gasped: seven monks
advanced in welcome, cooing like rock doves.
The ground was fire-grate ash, entirely barren;
reading looks, the eldest spoke to Brendan:

'We drink the dew. Our food arrives by raven,
one loaf one fish, our drop, our daily ration,
the bird so clockwork and plain bountiful.
Rest here, brothers. Come, observe our ritual.'

The monks performed a wordless parable:
seven stones in a fruit picker's pail,
bird-skin robes. Cried Brendan: 'Holy fathers,
bless you – these are quality palavers.'

The crew half-slept, that night, in golden cells,
their dreams hatchlings, their nerves eggshells.
Before the raven-dawn they fled in haste,
fearing their hosts' hunger, and their faith.

Interlude

Safe at sea and with full sail, the crew took their ease. Brother Michael dozed, a solid loaf, his head pillowed on a water bag. Brother Tom, sun-blushed, whittled a wooden cat figurine. Brendan sat whispering with brother Robert at the steering oar. Brother Colm kept his powder dry and said not a jot. Brother Aidan stroked his palm repeatedly across the leather cover of his voyage-book as though he were calming a horse without a herd. Brother Seamus did a chest-out strutting dance around the mast and flapped his elbows like a human bellows or a bird.

The Rock Saint

By dulcet winds the *Cog* was tickled west,
the crew pungent, their nostrils badly blessed.
A feature snared their view: a snag of rock,
a man, hairy as a bear, cross-legged on top.

Brendan hollered, 'Hoy! What game is this?'
The man replied: 'I perch. A steady business,
one hundred years and counting. Life is sweet.'
Brendan gave salute, as did the athlete.

Hellmouth

The weather fiercely dragonish
      with strong headwinds
the brothers' faith a cotton thread
      their minds bobbins

Ahead a coastline visible
      a scene most cruel
volcanic blast that feeds on air
      and human fuel

A packed crowd in that fiery pit
      who writhe and gurn
then some by detonation fly
      and fleck the sun

Devils with forks and leather flails
      maintain these lands
breeding horse-flies and leeches fat
      as Kerry lambs

Brendan spies a devil on shore
      and loudly cries
Who are these tortured kindling folks?
      What are their crimes?

The figure hocks up phlegm and yells
      Dead-eye loan sharks
crap-wigged kleptocratic bampots
      with shilling hearts

These parasites made profit off
poor citizens
their flesh is now a reddish clay
we fire their skins

A vile stench envelops the *Cog*
her retching crew
as terraced theatres of flame
slow-fade from view

The Siren

Brendan's lugs were tickled by a soundwave;
others heard it, gulped, and were enslaved:
a crooning moan of songlines, ghostly-fair
like whales in upper registers of air.

Brendan worked his lips but could not speak.
His crew lay round about, all spelled asleep,
the boat adrift, a punnet full of plums.
In dreams, they saw the starry eyes of loved ones.

Snore-surrounded, Brendan's heart grew sore.
He whispered, 'Heavenly Father, brooding Lord,
let phantoms wreak their wrath on me alone:
preserve my brothers; wing them safely home.'

The Stolen Bridle

Morning light. The brothers blinked, dumbstruck:
a temperate island, a jewelled castle of such work,
the roof iridescent as peacock feathers. Nearby,
four streams: of balsam, syrup, oil, and honey.

The crew began exploring, hushed but giddy.
Young brother Seamus, it was, whose glad eye
fell, enraptured, on the mouthwatering bridle,
its cheekpieces, throatlash, bit without parallel.

He stole this precious bridle, tucked in his habit.
He screamed, a second later, like a baby rabbit
clutched and raised heavenwards by a hawk –
devils took him; he knew fire, swallowed smoke.

Brendan prayed: 'Forgive our brother Seamus,
Lord; order those rank fiends to reunite us.'
Above, a falling star – no, a living ember:
Seamus crash-landed, hard, his flesh burnt umber.

The crew circled their stunned companion.
'Praise be to God,' cried Brendan. 'Speak, my son.'
Seamus rose, unsteady on his pins. A sick pup,
he grinned like one enlightened and threw up.

Devils' Mountain

The *Cog* under sail
    and fine progress
the helmsman angles her
    north-northwest

Injured brother Seamus
    yelps in his sleep
his blood fire-pricked
    his mind freaked

Unveiled up ahead
    a burning mountain
a figure on shore
    his mouth molten

He waves and hollers
    Brothers, welcome!
And you my delectable
    jug-eared Brendan

Ah devil cries Brendan
    you miserable shyster
away and arse-kiss
    your bright Master

The devil shouts back
    I want him I need
that Seamus-crisp
    that bridle thief

Deliver him Brendan
I'll fine-tune
his dissonant flesh
with fork and spoon

Seamus lies hidden
safe below thwarts
his guilt-stink
ripe as a corpse

Never! cries Brendan
the *Cog* about-turns
the mountain spews forth
a swarm of demons

Their clouds break
a rain of arrows
gobbets of lava
livid coals

Pull brothers pull!
with scooping oars
they flee those darts
those lively shores

Respite

The *Cog* beetled on, under full sail, a brisk westerly putting safe distance between her and flaming peril. The crew busied themselves with sewing kits, darning their injured woollens, patching their fire-bitten cloaks. Brother Seamus was feverish, his brow a dew-spangled rose; brother Colm took herbs and oats, and pummelled, and applied a poultice, whistling all the while like a mistle thrush. Brother Aidan cut quills, and mumbled his memory of recent events the better to capture their pith and pip on a page.

Brendan's Vision

Midsummer's midnight, clear skies. The crew lay slumbering all about; even Seamus, whose fever had broken, was soaked in sleep. Tom twitched like a dreaming dog. Robert hummed insensible hums. Aidan, Colm and Michael made a pile. Only Brendan stood awake. He settled his mind upon the star fields, their seeded light.

As Brendan's meditation deepened, he steadied himself by leaning back on the mast. His eyeballs had pins and needles. The sky above the *Cog* undulated as though underwater, the air inhabited: a traffic of angels whose skin flashed like fish scales; their wings iridescent as peacock feathers; their brows broad as highland lakes, green-veined, mountain-mirroring; their eyes balefires; their mouths waterfalls; their hymns a variety of roars.

The procession passed, the air emptied. Brendan fixed his gaze upon the starlit horizon: the sky was a top jaw, the ocean a lower jaw, the whole a mighty oyster, shut tight. The horizon thickened, by degrees; the sky yawned upwards, the vast ocean sagged. Revealed inside, a pearl, moon-sized. Brendan knew, at last, the double paradise, its hidden fruit of marvellous worth.

From that pearl bed a multitude stirred and came tumbling into view. The crane, the wild boar, the barnacle goose. Piping dormice, fiddling sea-cats, jousting snails. Brendan's generous ears could hear the ten choirs at work: the choir of pipsqueaks, the choir of grunts contented, the choir of thrapple-whistles, the choir of low-booming skinbags, the choir of predator alarums, the choir of trumpets most heart-rending and tremendous, the choir of high whinnies, the choir of whoops, the choir of tik tik tok, the choir of air passing though the nostrils of all animals asleep.

And Brendan, unsteady, slid slowly onto his knees and wept sorely. The vision marked an end, he knew; the outward journey over. What perils of the deep could bring them low? The choirs would sing them home. He rose to his feet, tiptoed over bodies, and shook brother Robert on the shoulder:

'Helmsman, I have seen the oyster and the pearl of promise. More on that later. But quickly now, check stars and winds, and set our sail for Ireland.'

Many Fish

A pristine windless noon. The crew leaned overboard, agog:
in water clear as glass, a vast congregation of fish. Angler,
whalefish, ribbontail ray. Clingfish, lancet, merrygold butter-
fish. Cardinal, angel pinfish, dab. Hickory, hootie blowfish,
pelican sponge. Batfish, haberdash. Bathypolyamorous eels.
Guddlefish, boop boop, candlefish, whiff. Bristlenose catfish,
bottlenose dogfish. Diaphanous crappie, cutlass, dibble, flub.
Will o' the wisp fish, ghoul, scoobfish, pouting prink.

   'Aidan, write these down,' said Brendan. 'Spare no ink.'

The Turf Rider

The crew hunker down
     the currach wave-mired
bedrock of Ireland
     so sorely desired

The day's mad event
     keen Robert sees first
an old man riding
     a divot of earth

A divot of earth
     his weedy surfboard
his kingdom a clod
     and him the turf lord

Codger! cries Brendan
     what barnstorming sin
makes you a sea-sod
     your base bannock-thin?

The figure replies
     Jehovah-blown floods
engulfed my country
     its pagan bird gods

I'm saved on a scrap
     and thank high heaven
a body wants home
     I know you Brendan

A freshening breeze
        the surfer sails on
an inmate who scours
        the ocean's prison

His parting holler
        part-muffled by wind
Brendan hears *raven*
        the rest imagined

Judas

The *Cog* was driven east, her crew spent.
At last, a tooth of rock, one resident:
a naked man flame-grilled on one side,
his flipside blue and mortified by ice.

'Judas,' cried Brendan, 'by God's wounds
your motley suffering is old news.
I'll pray for one day's respite: human flesh
deserves a break, some festive tenderness.'

Judas howled, 'This rock is my *reward*.
On Sundays, here, I'm faithfully adored
by fire and ice. Tomorrow I'm dragged home:
Hell's hooks, Hell's dark, Hell's grindstone.'

Burning Birds

A stalk of black smoke appeared on the horizon. At Brendan's word, the helmsman steered in that direction. In view, a rocky coast, a billowing cloud of debris and embers rising out of a fiery mountain. Closer, Brendan could see the cloud was birds, a vast murmuration, each one aflame. Their pitiful keening cries were too much to bear: the crew stopped their ears or shivered full-bodied like dogs shaking off water. And closer, the mountain's double nature was revealed: on one side a stream of boiling tar; on the other, a stream ice-cold and a wind so fierce and frigid the bark split from the trees to make a forest of standing nudes. Brendan prayed again for the dual-tormented grilled and frozen Judas, then ordered his crew to man the oars. As they rowed away from that place, a light rain of ash fell and speckled their clothes, bittered their lips.

Multum Bona Terra

Newfound land with safe harbour
      the whole crew on shore
topsoil-drunk and doing flings
      in fields of ripe corn

Sea-fatigue withdraws in waves
      a fertile country
no farmhands in evidence
      but fruiting bounty

And there a mile-high mountain
      where ravens prattle
and sun-flashed on southern flanks
      a corn-gold castle

Brothers hike to its threshold
      but guarding those gates
a nest of seething dragons
      irascible snakes

Brendan commands them *Hush now*
      and quit your station
quite abashed they slither off
      the entrance open

Interior crystal walls
      with creatures inlaid
their bodies of reddest bronze
      all silvery-veined

And suddenly those forms twitch
       from slumber to life
a wild stampede a show-reel
       confounding belief

Cockatrice roebuck panther
       a horn's *cri de cœur*
huntsmen on horse with sighthounds
       pursuing wild boar

The blood in brother Seamus
       drops below zero
Brendan here's a curse or else
       a heaven below

The abbot replies *My son*
       don't question this scene
cockatrice roebuck panther
       a castle can dream

The Walserands

The crew fled Weirdly Castle via cornfields,
again set sail. On shore, unholy squeals –
creatures in hot pursuit with bows and arrows,
their bodies a hotchpotch of odd bedfellows:

cranes' necks, top-heavy with boars' heads;
human torsos lurching on dogs' hind legs.
Brendan cried, 'You hairy mixter-maxters!
Do you know God? Confess! You cannot catch us.'

One beast replied, 'We knew Him, face to face:
as angels we lived in Heaven's choiring grace.
When Lucifer stirred rebellion we lay low,
hung neutral – our punishment this freak show.

Join us in exile, stay: we own a paradise,
and call that castle home. Just feast your eyes.'
In old seraphic dialects they growled
something about food, something about gold.

The Sea Leaf

A sleepy-sea dawn
    Robert yells weirdly
pointing starboard
    some queer debris

A cricket-sized man
    afloat on a leaf
Heaven's low trick
    or devil's mischief

In the ocean he dips
    a cut quill
decanting each drop
    into a thimble

Each thimbleful
    he tips and empties
Brendan he whispers
    I measure the seas

I measure the seas
    tara-loo tara-lay
by quill and by cup
    I'll finish by doomsday

Says Brendan *O speck!*
    you nugget!
this aim is a nonsense
    away and forget it

The tiny reply
  My seedless abbot
stars roll around
  like beans in a pot

By grains and feathers
  the infinite's weighed
Brendan sighs *Aye*
  the leaf bobs away

The Sea Serpent

A storm blew up. The troubled sea gave birth:
a snaky monster breasted the wave-surge,
encircled the *Cog*, chomped on its own tail
in play or hellish malice – none could tell.

Trapped in that ring, the boat was madly thrown;
Brendan loved the ride, from trough to crown.
His crew were not so blithe or God-uplifted:
belly contents mirrored faith, and shifted.

Insouciant Brendan prayed: 'Mindful Lord,
deliver us from this beast, cathedral-jawed.
Its dark idea of fun will drag us down.
Undoom this moment; let us live, not drown.'

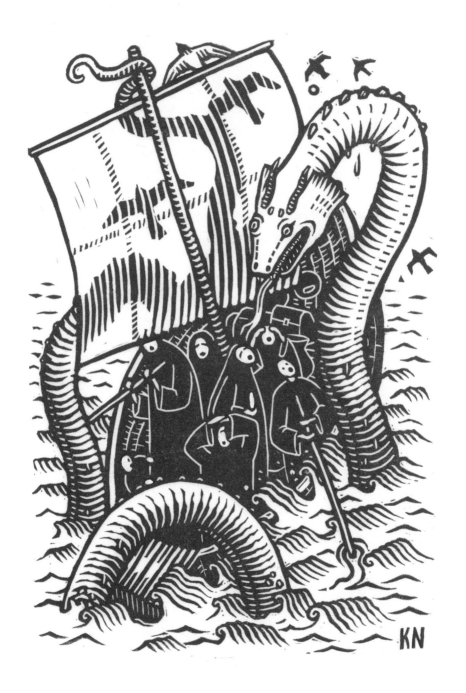

A World Below

The *Cog* flew east, outrunning pirate serpents of boisterous jaw. At length, becalmed, the crew took their breath. The air was a blue pool, thrown-stone-rippled; the water like heat-hazed air. A thin place, Brendan knew, not here nor there. A smatter of sound, as though from near-below: dog barks, market bustle, birdsong a raven's bill-whisker away, priestly bells, eightsome reels, close and clear as day, and yet unseen.

Robert plumbed the mirror-deep with rope and stone, struck bottom. The anchor was dropped, held fast, secure like a sheep in shearers' hands or the linchpin of an armlock in a whirling country dance.

The New Book

Brendan sidled up to brother Aidan.
'Scribe,' he said, 'are all your scratchings done?
Our journey saved in badger-bristle detail,
every scrap, scrape, nape-tingling miracle?'

Aidan nodded. 'Yes, the book's complete,
arse to nostrils, comb to cockerel's feet:
the sentient isle, *Jasconius* the whale;
the lass with hairy torso plus a tail;

hells where souls burned or sky-rocketed;
the bridle our soft Seamus pocketed;
the tortured Sunday holidays of Judas;
the boar's-head angels who pursued us;

the speck who measured oceans with a cup;
the serpent...' Brendan sighed, 'That's it, enough.
Our anchor's stuck below – so cut the rope!
I hear the choirs: let fortune marry hope.'

Home

The *Cog* rubs her leather belly
      on Kerry sand
the crew overspill and fish-flop
      they cannot stand

Fabulous now with legs like birds
      chicken-scrawny
a tribe unsprung all muscle gone
      nine years at sea

Hairy as saints who perch on rocks
      digesting airs
hairy as mermayds badly beached
      hairy as bears

Greeted as kings by shoreline dogs
      nosing high reek
flesh and clothes one greasy woven
      charnel-fabric

They hitch a ride in tradesmen's carts
      back to Ardfert
a welcome there of shocks and wails
      and full heartburst

Brendan carries Aidan's fat book
      as though a babe
lays it down on the altar cloth
      white as a wave

The crew are restored in wild rose-
            petalled water
sunset brings a clamour of crows
            then sleep's fortune

Brendan retires flower-festooned
            alone at last
his mind an oakwood of owl hoots
            and rooting masts

He listens wide-eyed his weak heart
            shifting like snow
an angel bright as springtime says
            It's time to go

Burial

Brendan was in the ground seven days when the crew gathered again. They stood around the *Cog*, her mast removed, her skin puckered and wrinkled after nine years at sea. Brother Robert made a circuit of her full extent, pressing his hand on each loved surface, tucking-in pieces of loose leather. Brother Tom took his final reading of her every grain, every knot, every ding and dent. Brother Aidan chanted her names aloud: Storm Garland, Harm Shield, Heal Fort, Wavehound, Crew Haven, Sea Home, Star Basket.

The six brothers bore the boat on their shoulders and made a slow march into the great wood. In a clearing they dug a broad pit, carolled by blackbirds. Brother Colm, very quietly, repeated the names of the seven noble varieties of tree as a word-charm: *daur, coll, cuilenn, ibar, uinnius, ochtach, aball.* Broad Brother Michael supported Brother Seamus, whose hellfire-wounds had not fully mended. The *Cog* was lowered in by ropes and blessed before the many spadefuls fell, her form vanishing into the dark hospitable seeding deep of Ireland.

NOTES

Introductions

In 1985, during my second year as an undergraduate at the University of Edinburgh, I bought an album by the Irish composer Shaun Davey: *The Brendan Voyage* (Tara, 1980). Subtitled 'an orchestral suite for uilleann pipes', it features the great piper Liam O'Flynn.

The Brendan in question is the sixth-century seafaring saint, 'Brendan the Navigator', but the musical themes of Davey's suite have their source in a more recent adventure. In 1976, the English author and explorer Tim Severin sailed from the west coast of Ireland to Newfoundland in a wooden-framed, leather-skinned boat, with stops at the Faroes and Iceland en route. His aim was to prove that St Brendan could well have made such a journey across the Atlantic in a similar vessel, as some legends have it, and that those landscapes are traceable in the early medieval myths. Severin's account of that incredible feat, *The Brendan Voyage*, was published in 1978.

In 2012 I began a Creative Writing PhD at Sheffield Hallam University, researching contemporary poetry on the subject of polar exploration, and the figure of St Brendan appeared in Barry Lopez's *Arctic Dreams*:

> Reading loosely, it is possible to imagine that Brendan reached the Faroes and Iceland, and perhaps saw the towering volcanic peak of Beerenburg on the eastern end of Jan Mayen Island. At one point the monks saw an iceberg that took three days of hard rowing to reach. Transfixed by its beauty, Brendan suggested they row through a hole in it, which in the evening light seemed 'like the eye of God'. (p. 316)

After following this lead back to the early Brendan texts, I saw an opportunity to make the saint's voyages the centre of the PhD's creative element – a grand narrative which would provide a framework for a book-length project, and reflect the perilous idealism of the Heroic Age of polar adventuring.

In the summer of 2015 I was fortunate enough to spend two weeks on the barquentine *Antigua*, sailing around Svalbard in the dazzling twenty-four-hour sunshine with a group of international artists. That experience of life aboard ship in a mind-altering landscape had a profound influence on this work, and I am grateful to the crew, the guides, and my fellow travellers.

The first draft of this book is included in my thesis *The Polar Sublime in Contemporary Poetry of Arctic and Antarctic Exploration* (Sheffield Hallam University, 2015).

The founding texts

St Brendan's biography was first composed towards the end of the eighth century, in a text now referred to as the *Vita Brendani* ('Life of Brendan'). It survives in seven versions, five in Latin and two in Irish, in manuscripts dating from the fourteenth and fifteenth century. The *Vita* tells us that Brendan (born circa 484 AD) was the son of Finnlug and Cara, and that his family were of the Altraige tribe who inhabited the lands around Tralee, Co. Kerry. As was traditional, he was fostered out for his education. He took holy orders, conversed with ministering angels, and, in saintly fashion, performed a variety of miracles. While meditating upon Sliabh Daidche (i.e. Mount Brandon, on the Dingle peninsula) and considering the 'mighty intolerable ocean', he was struck by a vision of a paradisal island and straightaway ordered three ships to be built. Thus began years of voyaging at sea, during which many marvels were encountered, and the Land of Promise found.

In tandem with this earliest material another text was written, in Latin, by Irish monks: the *Navigatio Sancti Brendani Abbatis* ('The Voyage of the Holy Abbot St Brendan'). Scholars date composition to the early or mid-ninth century. This is the tale that is now most commonly available in English translation (e.g. Webb 1965, O'Meara 1981), in which Brendan orders a single wooden-framed boat to be built, covered with tanned ox-hides and smeared with fat – a vessel known in Ireland as a currach. With seventeen monks, he sets sail for the Land of Promise. Notable stops on their journey include an island of giant sheep, an island which turns out to be a whale, a paradise of white birds, and a volcanic island of devils. They encounter isolated religious communities, hermits, and a tortured Judas Iscariot. The journey is circular and repetitive: they return to the same islands every year for seven years (including the accommodating whale) to celebrate the same events in the Christian calendar. Finally, the Promised Land of the Saints is found. A few happy days are spent there, and Brendan quickly dies on their return to Ireland.

Contemporaneous with the *Navigatio* were the secular Irish works known as *immrama* ('rowings', sea voyages) and *echtrae* ('outings', adventures, particularly to a magical Otherworld). The *immram* of *Mael Dúin* includes stops at various islands on which monstrous animals are found, mysterious native communities offer bounties or threats, and hermits dressed in nothing but their own hair give thanks to God for their survival on meagre rations. Stokes (1888) suggests that the *Navigatio* served as the inspiration for much of *Mael Dúin*, while other scholars believe it was the other way round. Mael Dúin is a warrior-hero in the mould of secular works such as the *Táin Bó Cúailnge*, and his journey is defined by a hell-for-leather sensationalism rather than moral instruction. Brendan's journey, from the start, has provided authors with an opportunity to exercise the imagination: it is an odyssey defined by sublime fictions.

European alternatives

The popularity of the *Navigatio* spread throughout Europe, and new interpretations appeared. The Anglo-Norman version, written during the reign of Henry I (1100–1135), took the Latin prose original as the basis for a poem of 1,840 octosyllabic lines, all of them rhyming couplets.

In the same period, circa 1150, a version is believed to have been written in the region of the Lower Rhine – 'believed', since no manuscript survives, and its existence is inferred by a variety of later texts which strongly suggest a common ancestor: two in Middle Dutch in verse, one Middle High German and one Middle Low German in verse, and one Middle High German prose text, all dating from around the fourteenth century. These texts are the focus of Clara Strijbosch's book *The Seafaring Saint*, and she suggests a wide range of influences at work in their creation: knowledge of the *Vita*, the *Navigatio* and *Mael Dúin* is in evidence, but there is also an echo of the twelfth-century German poem *Herzog Ernst* in which the titular hero travels through the Orient and encounters various wonders of the East. In one episode, Ernst and his companion encounter a group of men and women wearing costly silks, carrying bows and arrows, but their heads and necks are those of cranes. Similar-looking figures appear in the Germanic Brendan tales.

In these versions the motivation for Brendan's sea voyage is radically different. There is no longer a Promised Land of the Saints to be quested for; instead, Brendan becomes frustrated with the fantastical contents of old books (two paradises above the earth, huge islands in the sea, fish with forests on their back), refuses to believe what he has not seen with his own eyes, curses the author of one particular book, and throws it on the fire. An angel swiftly appears, and declares: 'All right, let the book burn; you will soon learn whether it was true or false. Jesus Christ commands you to sail the seas for nine years; then you will discover what is true and what is not' (Barron and Burgess 2005, p. 107). The voyage, then, is Brendan's penance for this evil deed, and his lack of faith in the fantastic truths of literature.

This *Voyage*

For its core episodes, I have based this book on the Middle Dutch versions referred to above; specifically, the Comburg manuscript, *Van Sente Brandane*, dating from around 1400. It comprises 2,284 lines, composed in rhyming couplets. I have taken the prose translation by Willem P. Gerritsen and Peter K. King in Barron and Burgess's *The Voyage of Saint Brendan* (p. 103–130) as my guide. Additional material has been sourced from or inspired by the books listed in the Select Bibliography.

Given that these poems arose from research into polar exploration, I felt that Brendan's anonymous crew of monks had to be identified and characterised if they were to play an effective part in the narrative. The Terra Nova expedition to Antarctica in 1910–1913 is as much the story of Lawrence Oates, Henry 'Birdie' Bowers and Edward Wilson (and many notable others, not least Kerryman Tom Crean) as it is of Robert Falcon Scott.

Likewise, it was not possible to write about a sea voyage without naming the vessel. The *Fram*, the *James Caird*,

Endurance, *Erebus* and *Terror* – they are essential lead characters in their respective tales. Reading the fourteenth-century Venetian version of Brendan (Barron and Burgess 2005, p. 168), I found the following description of the building of the boat: 'They made it very strong and all of wood, according to the way in which they built boats in that country; and he [Brendan] called it a cog.' The notes (p. 350) clarify as follows: 'The *coca* or *cocha* ('cog') was a type of merchant ship which was widely used by the Venetians from the thirteenth century onwards.' The similarity between Venetian *cocha* and Irish *currach* was striking, and I decided to name Brendan's boat the *Cog*. The poem 'The Building of the Boat' draws heavily on chapters two and three of Tim Severin's *The Brendan Voyage* for its details, and for the idea of a boat burial I am indebted to a presentation given by the Spanish artist Tito Perez Mora on board the *Antigua* in Svalbard, June 2015.

Form

With the Anglo-Norman and Middle Dutch Brendans both written in rhyming couplets, and given the history of heroic couplets in epic verse in English, it seemed at first the most obvious choice for these poems. On the other hand, a book-length narrative in this one form ran the danger of sounding like too much hammer, not enough harp.

I found a way ahead with the 2014 publication of *The Finest Music: Early Irish Lyrics*. Edited by the poet Maurice Riordan, one of my PhD supervisors at Sheffield Hallam University, it was my first (and very late) introduction to Irish poems written between the seventh and twelfth centuries. In particular, the 'otherworld' translations by Ciaran Carson provided an inspiring lead. The short four-line stanza form, rhyming ABCB, became the counterpoint to the couplet approach.

These lyric-shaped poems are set in the present tense, as an attempt to add forward momentum to a form which naturally tends towards the reflective rather than the epic. In the main I have used syllabic forms common in early Irish poetry: 5,5,5,5 ('The Great Fish', 'The Turf Rider'); 7,5,7,5 ('Multum Bona Terra'); 8,4,8,4 ('Hellmouth', 'Home').

Lastly, given that early Irish literature regularly features a mixture of prose and poetry (*Buile Suibhne*, *The Voyage of Bran*, *The Táin*), it seemed appropriate to add prose passages throughout this work.

Other Brendans

Given the enduring popularity of Brendan's tale, surprisingly few attempts have been made to put his story into contemporary verse. Denis Florence MacCarthy's 'The Voyage of St Brendan', included in his *Poems* of 1882, is very much of its time:

Such was the land for man's enjoyment made,
When from this troubled life his soul doth wend:
Such was the land through which entranced we strayed,
For fifteen days, nor reached its bound nor end.
Onward we wandered in a blissful dream,
Nor thought of food, nor needed earthly rest;
Until, at length, we reached a mighty stream,
Whose broad bright waves flowed from the east to west.

It is epic enough in its intentions, at ninety-two eight-line stanzas, though he concentrates on only a few of the traditional voyage episodes.

The one contemporary full-length treatment is Brendan Galvin's *Saints in Their Ox-hide Boat*. He names Brendan's crew members (five in total), and there is plenty of lively conversation between them and their Abbot. Galvin makes Brendan the first-person narrator, and his approach is informed by both the *Navigatio* and Tim Severin's 1976–1977 voyage from Ireland to Newfoundland via the high North:

> Had I in the flesh the ice cattle I've seen
> through mist, I'd be king of all Munster;
> Bishop of Rome if I ruled over half
> the ice clochans and oratories we outsteered
> while our hull plowed the slush mumbling
> and crackling against it, at times sounding
> like an invisible host whose boundaries
> we had violated, muttering one long
> threat against the boatskin

It is a spirited and satisfying account, mixing low and high registers, full of well-researched detail.

A special mention must go to George Mackay Brown's play 'The Voyage of St Brandon', first broadcast on BBC Radio 4 at Easter 1984. For his narrative framework he takes the version of the *Navigatio* published in William Caxton's *The Golden Legend*, 1483 (available in Barron and Burgess 2005, p. 323–343). Brown turns Brendan's visionary zeal into a dangerous form of delusion which puts him entirely at odds with the rest of the crew. Where Brendan sees a mighty hall with a feast laid out within, they see only a 'broken-down farm' and unappetising scraps:

> BRANDON   Now, Padraig, what can I help you to?
> Here's oysters.
> MALACHI Winkles. Winkles.
> BRANDON   And here's a sheep's heart. Truffles. Trout.
> I can recommend the broth – it's like unicorn's milk.
> MARTIN   Ugh! No, thank you, Brandon.
> BRANDON   The venison, then?
> MARTIN   It's only a bone. The dog might like it.

I won't give away the beautiful resolution to these differences in world-view. Brown finishes the play with an emphasis on the written word, and the importance of creative re-telling. To the scribe Brian, Brendan says:

> When they read your manuscript, they'll sneer. They'll say, *The Voyage of Brandon* indeed – a few seedless men in a salt waste, drifting from folly to folly [...] Never mind them. Imagine, say, a couple of country children on a roadside on a spring day. Tell the story of the voyage as if it was for their ears only.

It is advice I have kept in mind for my own version.

Select bibliography

Ashe, Geoffrey. *Land to the West: St Brendan's Voyage to America.* London: Collins, 1962.

Barron, W.R.J., and Burgess, Glyn S., eds. *The Voyage of Saint Brendan: Representative Versions of the Legend in English Translation with Indexes of Themes and Motifs from the Stories.* Exeter: University of Exeter Press, 2005.

Bitel, Lisa M. *Isle of the Saints: Monastic Settlement and Christian Community in Early Ireland.* Cork: Cork University Press, 1993.

Brown, George Mackay. *Three Plays:* The Loom of Light, The Well *and* The Voyage of Saint Brandon. London: Chatto & Windus, 1984.

Carson, Ciaran, trans. *The Táin: A New Translation of the Táin Bó Cúailnge.* London: Penguin Books, 2008.

Crotty, Patrick, ed. *The Penguin Book of Irish Poetry.* London: Penguin Books, 2012.

Flower, Robin. *The Irish Tradition.* Oxford: Clarendon Press, 1948.

Galvin, Brendan. *Saints in Their Ox-hide Boat.* Baton Rouge, LA: Louisiana State University Press, 1992.

Gerald of Wales. *The History and Topography of Ireland*, trans. John J. O'Meara. Harmondsworth: Penguin Books, 1982.

Heaney, Seamus. *Sweeney Astray.* London: Faber & Faber, 2001.

Kelly, Fergus. 'The Old Irish Tree-List'. *Celtica* (XI), 107–124, 1976.

Lehane, Brendan. *Early Celtic Christianity.* London: Continuum, 2005.

Little, George A. *Brendan the Navigator: An Interpretation.* Dublin: M.H. Gill & Son, 1945.

Lopez, Barry. *Arctic Dreams: Imagination and Desire in a Northern Landscape.* London: Macmillan, 1986.

Mackley, J.S., trans. *The Anglo-Norman Voyage of St Brendan.* Northampton: Isengrin, 2013.

Meyer, Kuno, trans. *The Voyage of Bran, Son of Febal, to the Land of the Living: An Old Irish Saga.* London: David Nutt, 1895.

Murphy, Gerard, ed., trans. *Early Irish Lyrics: Eighth to Twelfth Century.* Oxford: Clarendon Press, 1956.

Ó Cróinín, Dáibhí. *Early Medieval Ireland, 400–1200.* London: Longman, 1995.

O'Donoghue, Denis. *Brendaniana: St Brendan the Voyager in Story and Legend.* Dublin: Browne & Nolan, 1893.

O'Meara, John J., trans. *The Voyage of Saint Brendan: Journey to the Promised Land.* Portlaoise: The Dolmen Press, 1981.

Riordan, Maurice, ed. *The Finest Music: Early Irish Lyrics.* London: Faber & Faber, 2014.

Ryan, John. *Irish Monasticism: Origins and Early Development.* Dublin: Four Courts Press, 1992.

Severin, Tim. *The Brendan Voyage.* London: Hutchinson, 1978.

Squires, Geoffrey, ed., trans. *My News for You: Irish Poetry 600–1200.* Bristol: Shearsman Books, 2015.

Stokes, Whitley, trans. 'The Voyage of Mael Duin'. *Revue Celtique* (IX), 447–495, 1888.

———— *Lives of the Saints from the Book of Lismore.* Oxford: Clarendon Press, 1890.

Strijbosch, Clara. *The Seafaring Saint: Sources and Analogues of the Twelfth-century Voyage of Saint Brendan*. Dublin: Four Courts Press, 2000.

Webb, J.F., trans. *Lives of the Saints*. Harmondsworth: Penguin Books, 1965.